For Claudia, who has patiently and tenderly helped me to find my way back to wholeness,
and for William, who has protected me and taught me how to remain safe.
— R.D.

To Joh and the staff at ITC, for helping everyone stay safe, including me.
— S.S.

Library of Congress Cataloging-in-Publication Data is available.
Library of Congress Control Number: 2011912301

ISBN 978-0-9829938-6-6

14 13 12 11   1 2 3 4 5 6 7 8 9 10
Printed in the United States of America
First edition 2011

Little Pickle Press LLC
PO Box 983
Belvedere, CA 94920

Please visit us at www.littlepicklepress.com.

What Does It Mean To Be Safe?

By Rana DiOrio   Illustrated by Sandra Salsbury

Little Pickle Press

What does it mean to be safe?

Does it mean beating a throw to home plate? No.

Does it mean betting on a sure thing? No.

Does it mean locking yourself up? No!

Being safe means . . .

feeling secure in your environment
and protected from danger.

. . . looking both ways before you cross a street or parking lot.

. . . fastening your seat belt.

. . . using the buddy system when you swim or hike.

. . . being aware of your limits and honoring them.

. . . respecting the power of things that could harm you.

. . . knowing how to respond to emergencies.

. . . not tolerating bullying.

. . . not giving in to peer pressure.

. . . looking out for one another.

. . . learning what your rights are and making sure they are respected.

. . . listening to your inner voice.

. . . choosing your own beliefs and being accepted for who you are.

. . . not revealing information about yourself to strangers.

. . . telling an adult you trust when you feel uneasy.

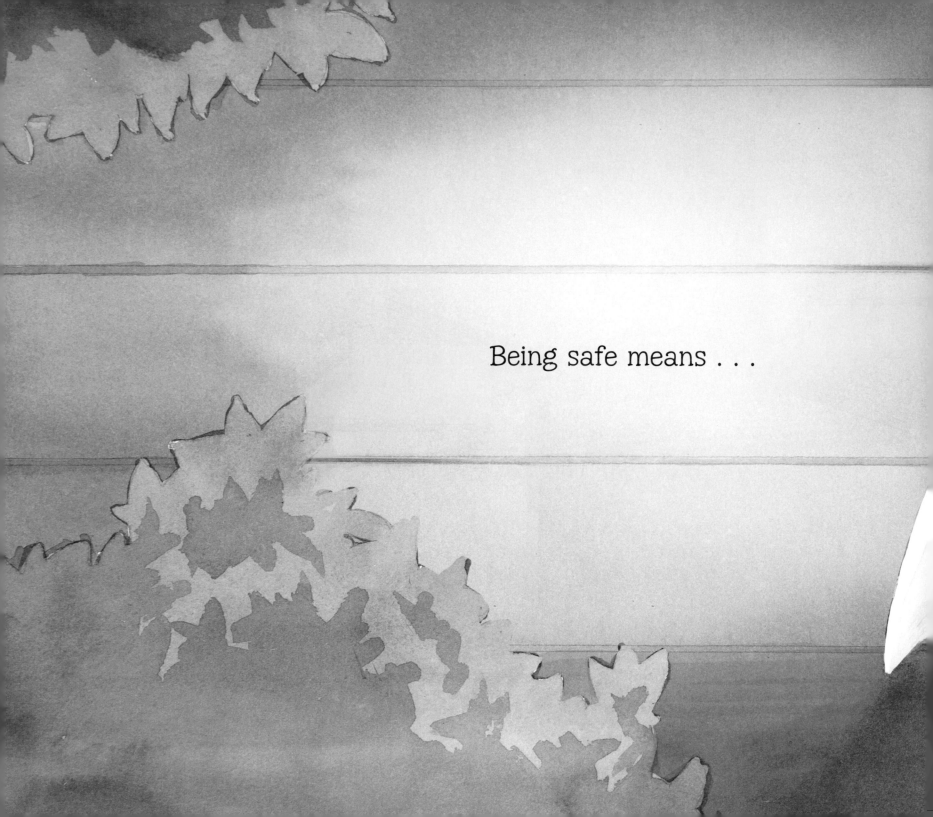

Being safe means . . .

realizing that you are the single best person
to protect your precious self.

So tell your friends what it means to be safe.

And spread the word—
when we're all safe,
our world is more peaceful
and joyful!

Our Mission

Little Pickle Press is dedicated to helping parents and educators cultivate conscious, responsible little people by stimulating explorations of the meaningful topics of their generation through a variety of media, technologies, and techniques.

To learn more about us, please visit www.littlepicklepress.com.

Little Pickle Press
Environmental Benefits Statement

This book is printed on **Appleton Utopia U2:XG Extra Green Paper.** It is made with extra (30%) PCRF (Post-Consumer Recovered Fiber) and Green Power. Green Power refers to electricity generated by renewable resources such as wind power, hydro, and biogas. It is FSC®-certified, acid-free, and ECF (Elemental Chlorine-Free).

Little Pickle Press saved the following resources in green paper, cartons, and boards:

Total Trees Saved	Total Energy Saved	Kilowatt-Hours Saved	Greenhouse Gas Reduction	Waste Water Reduction	Solid Waste Reduction
Post-consumer recovered fiber displaces wood fiber with savings translated as trees.	PCRF content displaces energy used to process equivalent virgin fiber.	Number of kilowatt-hours of electricity offset by purchase of renewable energy.	Measured in CO_2 equivalents, PCRF content and Green Power reduce greenhouse gas emissions.	PCRF content eliminates wastewater needed to process equivalent virgin fiber.	PCRF content eliminates solid waste generated by producing an equivalent amount of virgin fiber through the pulp and paper manufacturing process.
25.57 trees	**13.8 mil BTUs**	**4,190 kWh**	**9,788 lbs**	**15,180 gal**	**1,124 lbs**

FSC — MIX — Paper from responsible sources — FSC® C005259 — www.fsc.org

RAINFOREST ALLIANCE CERTIFIED

Green U Power

PRINTED WITH SOY INK™

Appleton Utopia U2:XG Extra Green is certified for the standards of Forest Stewardship Council™ by SmartWood, a program of the Rainforest Alliance. The above information is based on US EPA and Environmental Defense Fund calculations for total paper, board, and carton tonnage.

We print and distribute our materials in an environmentally-friendly manner, using recycled paper, soy inks, and green packaging.

Expert 8m
Beginners 3m
Pond 0.1m
River 1m

About the Author

It has taken Rana DiOrio over four decades of healing, learning, and growth to be in a position to write *What Does It Mean To Be Safe?*. Now, as the mother of three young children, she wants to show readers how they can protect themselves, and to encourage parents to be ever-mindful of their children's safety. "We all have an amazing capacity to discern when we are not safe," Rana explains. "As parents, we need to teach our children to trust their instincts, and to establish the boundaries necessary for them to thrive."

Rana has written her way through life—as a student, a lawyer, an investment banker, a private equity investor, and now as an author and publisher of award-winning children's media. Her interests include practicing yoga, reading non-fiction and children's books, dreaming, effecting positive change, and, of course, being global, green, present, and safe. She lives in Tiburon, California with her three Little Pickles.

About the Illustrator

Sandra Salsbury grew up in the redwood forests of the Santa Cruz Mountains in California. She received her BFA and MFA in illustration from the Academy of Art University in San Francisco. As well as illustrating, Sandra teaches art classes and works at her local schools.

When illustrating *What Does It Mean To Be Safe?*, Sandra thought about the time when she felt safest—as a child running through the forest, morning, noon, and night. "Being safe is not just about following rules, but also about being happy with who you are and the life you have," she says.

When she is not drawing, Sandra enjoys reading, hiking, cooking, and attempting to do yoga (with limited success). She still lives in the San Francisco Bay Area and often returns to the forests of her childhood for hiking and picnics.